The Little Book of Positive Affirmations

MATT VERRELL

DEDICATION

This Little Book is dedicated to my wife, Rowena, my family and all those people who want to make a difference in their lives – those who aren't afraid to take control of their destiny. We are all here for a reason and a purpose. We all have a responsibility to ourselves and our loved ones to fulfil that purpose and make every moment count. Have the courage to stand strong and let in life's avalanches of abundance.

Carpe Diem

NOTES TO THE READER

As you read through these positive affirmations, visualize what your life is now like with this affirmation in it. Imagine it is already so. How does it feel? What do you see around you? What colors do you see? I have decided these affirmations will start with the words "I am" – my goal is for these to be as helpful to you as they have been for me.

The more emotion you can attach to the affirmation, the more your subconscious mind will believe, through repetition, that it is already true, helping to change your life for the better.

I invite you to start at any page you like – it doesn't have to be at the beginning. The book should be seen as a reference as and when you need it. This is your book: make notes; include drawings; and let your imagination run wild and free.

If you can hold it in your head, you can hold it in your hand

Bob Proctor

Life: a tremendous opportunity

I AM

CREATING A MAGNIFICENT LIFE

Impressive: having the ability to awaken admiration, awe and respect

I AM

IMPRESSIVE

Infinite: to be immeasurably
great and unstoppable

I AM

INFINITE AND MY POSSIBILITIES ARE ENDLESS

Wonderful: to be excellent; great; marvellous

I AM

WONDERFUL

Wise: to have the power to judge what is true or right

I AM

WISE AND OTHERS VALUE MY CONTRIBUTION

Immeasurable: to be limitless

I AM

IMMEASURABLE

Joy: the emotion of great delight caused by something that is satisfying

I AM

PRODUCING ENDLESS JOY

Boundless: to be unlimited in your potential

I AM

BOUNDLESS

Happy: to be content with yourself and your surroundings

I AM

HAPPY WITH HOW MY LIFE IS UNFOLDING

Philanthropist: an individual who has concern for human welfare and advancement

I AM

A PHILANTHROPIST

Charitable: to be generous in donations or gifts to relieve the needs of ill or helpless persons or animals

I AM

CHARITABLE

Pleasure: the state or feeling of enjoyment or delight

I AM

A PLEASURE TO BE AROUND

Generous: to be free from smallness of mind and liberal in giving and sharing

I AM

GENEROUS

Integrity: adhering to moral
and ethical principles

I AM

INTEGRITY

Cheerful: to be in good spirits

I AM

CHEERFUL

Communicator: one skilled at conveying information and ideas to others

I AM

A BRILLIANT COMMUNICATOR

Genius: to have an exceptional, natural characteristic of intellect

I AM

A GENIUS

Energetic: to possess power in abundance

I AM

ENERGETIC

Courageous: the quality of mind and body that enables one to face difficulty without fear

I AM

COURAGEOUS

Bountiful: to be generous and abundant

I AM

BOUNTIFUL

Influence: the capacity or power of a person to produce effects on the actions, behaviours or opinions of others

I AM

A POSITIVE INFLUENCE TO ALL WHO KNOW ME

Strong: to exhibit mental and/or physical power

I AM

STRONG

Adventurous: willing to engage in exciting or unusual experiences

I AM

ADVENTUROUS

Leader: a guide to your fellow people

I AM

A WONDERFUL LEADER

Charismatic: to have a special gift or power that gives influence or authority over others

I AM

CHARISMATIC

Daring: to be bold and full of courage

I AM

DARING

Lively: being full of life and energy

I AM

LIVELY

Master: a person with the ability or power to use or control something

I AM

A MASTER OF SPEECH

Superb speaker: an illustrious conveyer of information through speech to others

I AM

A SUPERB SPEAKER

Outstanding: to be distinct, excellent and distinguished

I AM

OUTSTANDING

Healthy: possessing a sound and vigorous body and mind

I AM

HEALTHY

Wealthy: to be rich in character and material

I AM

WEALTHY

Prosperity: a successful, flourishing or thriving condition

I AM

CREATING MORE PROSPERITY IN MY LIFE

Financially prosperous:
someone who is well placed to
help others

I AM

FINANCIALLY PROSPEROUS

Understanding: knowledge and enlightened intelligence

I AM

TOTAL UNDERSTANDING

Brilliance: to be excellent and distinct

I AM

WALKING BRILLIANCE

Educated: to display the qualities of culture and learning

I AM

EDUCATED

Wisdom: knowledge of what is true or right coupled with just judgement

I AM

INFINITE WISDOM

Over-achiever: to perform above your potential

I AM

AN OVER-ACHIEVER

Abundant: an extremely plentiful supply of whatever you turn your mind to

I AM

ABUNDANT

Charming: to be pleasing or delightful

I AM

CHARMING

Fearless: to be without fear;
bold and brave

I AM

FEARLESS

Success: In the words of Ralph Waldo Emerson, "to laugh often and much; to win the respect of intelligent people and the affection of children; to earn the appreciation of honest critics and endure the betrayal of false friends; to appreciate beauty, to find the best in others; to leave the world a bit better, whether by a healthy child, a garden patch or a redeemed social condition; to know even one life has breathed easier because you have lived. This is to have succeeded."

I AM

A MASSIVE SUCCESS

Powerful: to have or exert a
great force

I AM

POWERFUL

Expansion: a state of growth

I AM

EXPANSION

Honest: being true in principle,
intention and action

I AM

HONEST

Control: you've got this – to be
the person you want to be

I AM

IN CONTROL OF MY LIFE

Magnificent: extraordinarily
fine and superb

I AM

MAGNIFICENT

Thankful: to feel or express gratitude

I AM

THANKFUL FOR THE OPPORTUNITIES I CREATE IN MY LIFE

Unique: simply look in the mirror

I AM

UNIQUE IN THIS WORLD

Significant: of importance and consequence

I AM

A SIGNIFICANT PART OF THE UNIVERSE

Individual: a person
distinguished from a group

I AM

AN INDIVIDUAL EXPRESSION OF A CREATIVE POWER

Enough: sufficient for a purpose

I AM

ENOUGH

Exceptional: to be unusual or
extraordinary

I AM

EXCEPTIONAL

Capable: having power and ability

I AM

CAPABLE OF ANYTHING I SET MY MIND TO

Ability: the power or capacity to do something or act in a particular way

I AM

CERTAIN OF MY ABILITY TO SUCCEED

Striving: to make strenuous
effort toward any goal

I AM

STRIVING TO BE THE BEST VERSION OF MYSELF

Experience: knowledge or practical wisdom gained from what one has observed or undergone

I AM

MORE EXPERIENCED
THAN I WAS YESTERDAY

Father: a positive influence on a child

I AM

AN INCREDIBLE FATHER

Mother: a positive influence on a child

I AM

AN INCREDIBLE MOTHER

Growing: becoming greater

I AM

GROWING EVERYDAY

Forward-thinking: planning for the future; forward-looking

I AM

FORWARD-THINKING

Supportive: providing help, information and encouragement to others

I AM

SUPPORTIVE

Greatness: considerable in power

I AM

PLANTING THE SEEDS OF GREATNESS IN THE GARDEN OF MY MIND

If I have seen further than others, it is by standing on the shoulders of giants

Sir Isaac Newton

I AM

STANDING ON THE
SHOULDERS OF GIANTS

ABOUT THE AUTHOR

Following a career as a lawyer in London, Matt Verrell was searching for greater meaning and purpose to his life. He became a full-time carer for individuals struggling with dementia, before expanding his care skills into end-of-life and palliative care. The privilege of working with individuals at the end of their lives gave him a passion to help those who have a lot of living to do. He is now on the path to become a Life Coach. He lives in Hertfordshire, England with his family.

Made in the USA
Middletown, DE
22 April 2023

29327967R00085